Igor Suvorov

It's Hard To Be a Russian Spy ...

The Great Collection Of Riddles & Brain Teasers From The Final Examination of Soviet and Russian Spies

D1411728

There's training to be an Olympic Athlete. Then there is training to a Russian Spy. Both extremely difficult and a much esteemed percentage of people around the world get to be picked for it. But there is no shadow of doubt which of these requires a person to be literally Jack of all trades- smart, cunning, highly intelligent, resilient and the perfect mix of brains and brawns.

There is an aura of mysticism surrounding Spies and very few people have told the tale of where it all began- in the training room. Put together by means that better remain cloaked, or perhaps a story for another time, author Igor Suvorov brings you a choice collection of fifty riddles and brain teasers that these Soviet and Russian spies had to clear in order to be deemed fit to be released to the field. Anyone can solve a riddle, but these are the riddles that only as few as 4% of untrained people will be able to solve!

As if that is not good enough, the person taking the exam has to clear 94% of all the presented questions. This is the holy grail of all spy brain teasers, a book that you can keep your brain sharp with, a tool with which you can spend endless hours poring over. Have you go what it takes? Time to find out!

It's not just hard to be a Russian Spy; it's VERY hard and only the sharpest mind will be one.

TOC

All images from openclipart.org

https://openclipart.org/unlimited-commercial-use-clipart

1. A Flock of Ducks

There was a flock of ducks flying in the sky. One ahead of the other two; one behind of the other two; one between the other two, and three in a row. How many ducks were flying?

Answer:

Three ducks were flying, one by one.

2. Two Fathers and Two Sons

On the way to Bombay two fathers and two sons happened to find three rupees (silver coins) lying in their path and divided them quickly – each of travellers receiving 1 coin. How did they manage to do it?

Answer:

The travellers managed to divide the coins evenly, because there were three of them: the grandfather, the father and the son (in other words – two fathers and two sons).

3. Family of Painters

Three painters had a brother – Ivan, but Ivan didn't have any brothers. How was this possible?

Answer:

The painters were sisters.

4. How to Divide?

How to divide 5 apples between 5 people so that each one gets an apple and 1 apple stays in the basket.

Answer:

One person takes a basket with an apple in.

5. Diophantus' Riddle

Try to find three numbers that add up to 20, 30 and 40 when you add them by pairs.

Answer:

The numbers are 5, 15 and 25.

6. Grandfather and Grandchildren

Grandfather bought nuts for his grandchildren. But before the feast he asked kids to divide the nuts into two parts so that the lesser part, when you quadruple it, was equal to the greater part, when you take a third of it. What are these parts?

Answer:

1 and 12 nuts. Any pair of whole numbers with a ratio 12 to 1 will be a correct answer.

7. 100 Pupils

A father decided to send his son to school and asked the teacher, "Tell me, how many pupils are there in your class?" The teacher answered, "If there comes as many pupils as I have now, and then a half as many, and then a quarter as many, and if your son also comes, then I will have 100 pupils." How many pupils were there in the class?

Answer: 36 pupils.

8. A Pitcher and a Glass

You have a pitcher filled with water and a crystal glass which should be filled to the brim with the water from the pitcher. But there is one condition: you should leave the same amount of water in the pitcher as there is now before your actions.

Answer:

It's just a piece of cake. Take the glass and put it carefully onto the pitcher's bottom without spilling a drop of water on the table.

9. Trains

On one of its sections a double-line railway dives down into a tunnel and turns into a single-line railway. There's no way for trains to pass each other. Last summer a train ran into the tunnel from the one side of it at full speed. Another train rushed headlong into the tunnel. No crash happened. Why?

Answer:

The trains ran into the tunnel at a different time.

10. Neighbors

Ali, Ben and Cyrill were born in 1309, 1310 and 1311 in one and the same city block of Jerusalem. They grew up and were living in one and the same place for the whole life. Each one has lived for 60 years, leading an active lifestyle, but they never saw each other. How could this happen?

Answer:

Ali was a Muslim, Ben was a Jew, Cyrill was a Christian. Ali was born in 1309 according to the Muslim Calendar. This calendar starts with the year 622 AD, when Muhammad migrated from Mecca to Medina. This means that the year 1309 in the Muslim Calendar corresponds to the year 1930 AD. Ben was born in 1310 according to the Hebrew Calendar that starts with the year 3761 BC. This means that Ben was born 3000 years earlier than Cyrill, who was born 619 years earlier than Ali.

P.S. There is another variant: they couldn't see each other because they were all blind.

11. Heart Attack

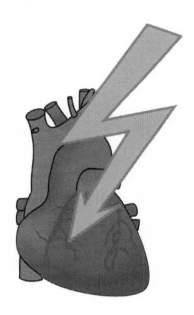

A man came home in the evening, shut off all the lights and went to sleep. He woke up in the morning, did exercises. Then he came to the window and looked out, after that the man had a heart attack.

Questions: What was the man's occupation? What did he see from the window?

Answer:

He was a lighthouse keeper, in the morning he saw wrecked ships.

12. A Remedy for Insomnia

A man was tossing and turning, he couldn't get asleep... Then he took his phone, dialed someone's number and heard a dial tone. After that he hung up and fell asleep. Question: why couldn't he get asleep?

Answer:

His neighbor was snoring loudly. The man called him, and the neighbor woke up.

13. Stop

A man left his car near a bank and went inside. He was keeping 25 people. Then he ran out of the bank with 200 dollars. A policeman who saw it all stopped him, rebuked him, and let him go. Why?

Answer:

When the man left his car in front of the bank, he hogged the road. That caused a traffic jam where 25 people got stuck. The policeman told the man not to leave his car in any places where it can hog the road.

14. Drunken Driver

Holidays were coming soon, so a police chief decided to reinforce the fight against drunken drivers. Under his order two officers were on duty near the only club in the centre of the town. They saw a man who seemed to be drunk leave the club and fall into the snow. In a few seconds he stood up and started to look for the key near his car. Finally he managed to start the car.

His car was constantly swerving. Policemen stopped him and asked him to blow into a breathalyzer. There was a negative result. Obviously, something was wrong with the breathalyzer, because the man smelled of alcohol. The policemen took him to the police department to make a test again. But the result was the same. The police were confused. Try to explain the situation.

Answer:

The man was sober, he was distracting the policemen while his drunken friends were driving home.

15. Races

A famous racing car driver was going to turn on the Formula 1 race track. Suddenly he broke abruptly and, having turned into a corner, he saw crashed cars on the track, they were situated dangerously on the race track. He couldn't have seen them before turning. The organizators hadn't warned him. There was no smoke, no fire, no smell that could have warned him about the accident. How could he know that there is danger around the turn and avoid crashing?

Answer:

Although the driver couldn't see what was going on, he saw people on the stands looking at something that was there. He understood that they were not looking at him, although he was so famous, because they saw something more interesting – maybe a crash that had happened around the turn.

16. A Boy and a Tree

A boy's height was 1 meter (3,3 ft.). He hammered a nail into a tree to mark his height. Three years later he came back to this place. The boy had grown by 20 centimeters, the tree had grown by 40 centimeters (1,3 ft.). How much higher was the nail comparing to the boy's height?

Answer:

The nail was lower by 20 centimeters (0,66 ft.) than the boy's height. The nail was at the same height since trees grow at their tops.

17. Love Triangle

A woman has a rich husband and a rich lover. They both are ready to buy any expensive things for her! But neither of them give her pocket money. However, the woman gets a good deal of money each time she gets a luxurious present. How is this possible?

Answer:

The woman makes both her husband and her lover buy the same presents for her. Then she returns the second present to the shop and gets money for it. So the husband thinks that it was him who gave her the present, and the lover believes that he gave it to her. The woman has the present (the first one) and money for the second one!

18. Chameleons

There were 13 red, 15 green, and 17 blue chameleons on an island. When two chameleons of two different colours meet each other, they change their colours to the third one all at the same time (for example, a blue one and a green one change their colours to red).

Is it possible that after a while all chameleons will have the same colour?

Answer:

It is impossible, because the numbers 13, 15, 17 have different remainders of division by 3.

19. Speculator

A man bought a car for 650 dollars, then he sold it for 725 dollars. After that he thought that he had sold himself short, so he bought the car again for 750 dollars, but this time he sold it for 725 dollars. Did he lose his money or gain some in the result?

Answer:

He gained 50 dollars.

20. Socks

A man has 3 white, 3 black, 3 pink, and 3 blue socks in his dresser. What is the minimum number of the socks he should take out of the dresser to make 3 pairs of them, if he can't see their colour?

Answer: 9.

21. Accusation

Three men: Ivanov, Petrov, and Sidorov came up for trial. They were charged for a robbery.

The investigation has found out that:

If Ivanov is not guilty, or Petrov is guilty, then Sidorov is not guilty.

If Ivanov is not guilty, Sidorov is not guilty.

Is Ivanov guilty?

Answer:

Ivanov is guilty.

22. Three Clowns

Clowns Bam, Bim and Bom came into the arena. They were dressed in red, blue and green shirts. Their shoes had the same colours. Bim's shoes and shirt were the same colour. Bom wasn't wearing anything red. Bam's shoes were green, whereas his shirt wasn't. Which colours are Bom's and Bim's shoes and shirts?

Answer:

Bam's shirt is blue, Bom's shirt is green.

Bom's shoes can't be red or green (because Bam has green shoes).

As far as Bam's shoes are green, Bom's shoes can't be red or green. This means they are blue. Bim has red shoes left. That's why his shirt is also red. Then Bam's shirt is blue, Bom's shirt is green.

23. Flour, Groats and Sugar

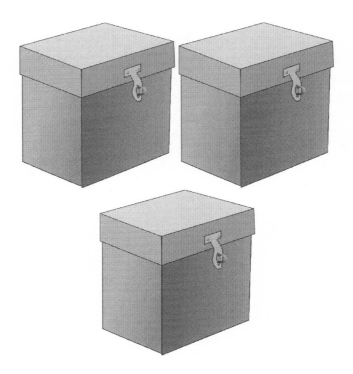

There are flour, groats and sugar in three boxes. "Groats" is written on the first one, "Flour" – on the second one, "Groats or Sugar" – on the third one. None of the written is true for the products contained in any box. What is in each box?

Answer:

Sugar is in the first box, groats is in the second one, flour is in the third one.

There isn't groats or sugar in the third box. Therefore, it has flour in it.

It's not groats in the first box. But it's also not flour, because flour's in the third one. This means that it's sugar in the first box. Then there is groats (the only product left) in the second one.

24. Where Is What?

There are milk, lemonade, kvass and water in a bottle, a glass, a pitcher and a jar. Water and milk are not in the bottle, a vessel with lemonade is between the pitcher and a vessel with kvass, it's neither lemonade nor water in the jar. The glass is near the jar and the vessel with milk. Which drink is in which vessel?

Answer:

Milk is in the pitcher, lemonade is in the bottle, kvass is in the jar, water is in the glass.

25. A Boy and a Girl

There are a boy and a girl.

"I'm a boy," says a black-haired child.

"I'm a girl," says a red-haired child.

If at least one of them lies, then who's a boy and who's a girl?

Answer:

The boy is red-haired and the girl is black-haired.

26. Numbers on Foreheads

Two sages were told that tomorrow they will have to stand in front of each other and each one will have numbers 1 or 2 on their foreheads (they both can have the same number). Each of them should guess what is the number on his forehead and write this number on a piece of paper. How should the sages act so that at least one of them could guess the number right? (during the experiment it is not allowed to talk, make signals etc.)

Answer:

Before the experiment the sages agree that the first one writes the number written on the second one's forehead, the second one writes the number opposite to the one that's written on the first one's forehead.

27. Three Envelopes

You have three envelopes and you have to eat one of them immediately. There is a piece of paper with two statements in each envelope. Both statements are true in one of the envelopes, both statements are false in another one, and there is one true statement and one false in the third envelope. Here are the statements:

Envelope 1:

1. You shouldn't eat this envelope.

2. You have to eat the second envelope.

Envelope 2:

1. You shouldn't eat the first envelope.

2. Eat the third envelope.

Envelope 3.

1. Don't eat this envelope.

2. Eat the first envelope.

So which envelope should you eat?

Answer:

You should eat the third envelope.

28. Paradox of the Heap

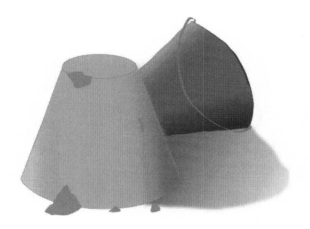

Two friends met each other in the street. They were talking when suddenly one of them saw a heap of sand.

"Can you see this heap of sand? It doesn't exist actually," he said.

"Why?" his friend asked him.

"It's easy. One sand grain does not make a heap of sand. If n sand grains can't make a heap of sand, than even after adding one more sand grain they still can't make a heap. This means that no number of sand grains can make a heap, consequently, there is no heap of sand."

Answer:

This is the Paradox of the Heap. The man used the principle of complete induction. But you can't use the same principle in similar riddles, because the notion 'a heap of sand' is not defined there.

29. Eyes

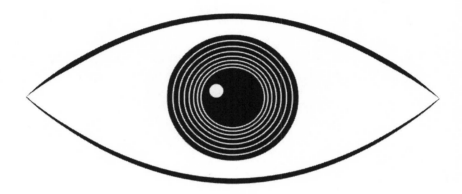

You don't have to have eyes to be able to see. We can see without the right eye. And we can see without the left eye. As far as we don't have any other eyes, this means that none of the eyes is necessary to be able to see. Is this statement true? If not, what is a mistake here?

Answer:

In this riddle the statement "We can see without the right eye. And we can see without the left eye" is supposed to mean "none of the eyes is necessary to be able to see", so there is a premise, "We can see without the right eye which means the right eye is not necessary". The premise is false, but the riddle says it's obvious. That is the mistake.

30. Locks and Keys

There are 10 closed locks and 10 similar keys for them. Each lock can be opened only with one key, but the keys are all in a muddle. Let's take a lock, call it "the first one" and try to open it with each of the 10 keys. If we are lucky, it will be opened with the first key, or with the tenth one – if we aren't.

How many times should we try to find the key at worst to open all the locks?

Answer:

It's enough to try 9 times for the first lock (the tenth is not necessary), for the second one it would be 8 times, for the third one – 7 times etc., and for the last lock left we don't need to try to find the key at all. So we'd need to try 45 times (9+8+7+...+1+0 = 45).

31. How Many Interpreters?

10 delegates who do not understand each other's languages came to an international conference. What is the minimum number of interpreters needed for the conference if each interpreter speaks only 2 languages?

Answer: 9.

32. 70 Balls

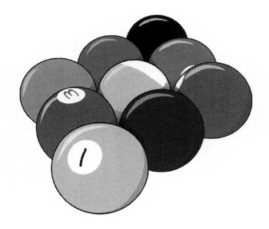

There are 70 balls in a box: 20 of them are red, 20 – blue, 20 – yellow, all the rest are black and white. What is the minimum number of balls you should take without seeing them so that there are at least 10 balls of the same colour?

Answer: 38.

33. Hole in a Pocket

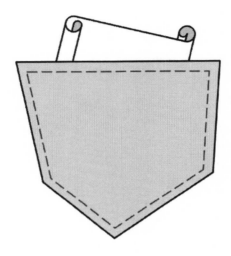

There are 10 coins in your pocket – 49 cents in total. You're walking with your friend Henry, who has the same sum of money in his pocket. Suddenly one coin falls out of someone's pocket – yours or Henry's. What are the chances that it was a ten cent coin?

Answer:

If your friend and you have 10 coins that are 49 cents in total, there should be four one cent coins, three ten cent coins and three five cent coins. This means that you and your friend have six ten cent coins out of twenty coins. So there is a 30% chance that it was a ten cent coin (6 out of 20).

34. Age

A man was 20 years old in 1970, but he was only 15 years old in 1975. Is this possible?

Answer:

It's possible if the man was living in the BC era.

35. First Birthday

A girl celebrated her birthday for the first time when she turned 8 years old.

Why?

Answer:

Answer: The girl was born on February 29th,1896, but 1900 was not a leap year, because the end-of-century years are leap years only when the number of centuries is divisible by 4. That's why after she was born the 29th of February came for the first time only in 1904 when she turned 8 years old. On next birthday she turned 12 years old.

36. Reserve Player

36 players (4 of them are reserve players) play a game that lasts 15 minutes. Reserve players replace each player by turns, so all the players spend the same amount of time on the ground. How much time do they spend there?

Answer:

13,5 minutes: (15*36)/40 = 13,5

37. Newborn's Weight

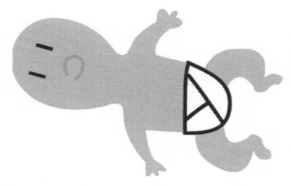

A mother asked, "What is the weight of my newborn baby?" A nurse answered, "12.96 pounds divided by 1/4 of his own weight." What was the baby's weight?

Answer:

7.2 pounds.

12.96:1.8 = 7.2

38. Accumulators

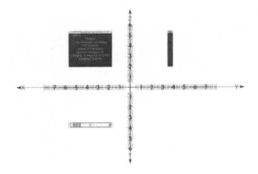

There is 10% of accumulators which are defective in daily production volume. If you take 3 randomly chosen accumulators, what are the chances that all three of them are defective?

Answer:

0.1 * 0.1 * 0.1 = 0.001. One chance in a thousand.

39. Easter Egg

There is a toy inside an Easter egg. A buyer asked a seller if he could buy a toy without an egg. The seller answered that an egg with a toy inside costs 4.5 dollars, an egg without a toy costs 4 dollars more than a toy. How much should the buyer pay for the toy?

Answer:

The toy costs 25 cents, the egg costs 4 dollars and 25 cents, so it costs 4 dollars more than the toy.

40. Apple Garden

There are 100 apples in a row at distances of 1 meter from each other. A gardener put a basket at a distance of one meter from the first apple. How long will his way be if he decides to pick the apples one by one and go back to the basket to put each one separately there (the basket is on the same place for the whole process)?

Answer:

He has to come to each apple and go back to the basket. This means that the number of the meters will be equal to the doubled sum of the first 100 numbers, or 101 when increased a hundredfold (10 100). This is more than 100 kilometers. This way of picking is quite tiresome!

41. A Hunter and a Shepherd

A hunter met two shepherds. One of them had 3 loaves of bread, another one had 5 loaves. All the loaves had the same size. The three men divided the bread equally and ate it. Then the hunter gave them 8 coins. How should the shepherds divide the money?

Answer:

The first one should get 1 coin, the second one gets 7 coins, because each one ate 2 2/3 loaves of bread. That's why the first shepherd gave the hunter only 1/3 loaf, the other one gave him 2 1/3 loaves (1/3 and 7/3).

42. Prices for a Cow and a Horse

Ranchman offered a cowboy to buy 4 cows and 3 horses for 370 dollars or 3 cows and 4 horses for 330 dollars.

How much will 1 cow and 1 horse cost?

Answer:

One horse costs 30 dollars, one cow costs 70 dollars.

43. Automobile Dealership

An automobile dealership's owner has sold two cars, with a 10% profit for the first one and a 10% loss for the second one. In the result the owner has got a 5% profit. At what price had the owner bought the cars if the profit was 1 000 dollars?

Answer:

The owner bought the first car for 15 000 dollars and the second one for 5 000 dollars. So the profit was 1 500 dollars, the loss was 500 dollars. A clear profit was 1 000 dollars or 5%.

44. How Many Steps Are There On an Escalator?

A man was getting late to work and he ran down a metro escalator, to make up for the time wasted in a traffic jam. While he was going down at a speed of 2 steps a second he counted 140 steps. The next day he was in the same situation, but this time he could come to work even later. Of course, he was running faster down the same escalator – at a speed of 3 steps a second, but this time he counted 28 steps more than before.

It was strange: the faster you run, the longer the escalator is.

How many steps are there on the escalator?

Answer:

The escalator has 280 steps.

If we say that the total number of steps on the escalator is N, then N is the number of the steps the escalator itself has run, plus the number of steps the man made on it. In the first case the amount the time was 140 : 2 = 70 seconds, in the second case it was 56 seconds. If the escalator has uniform speed, then we can write the following equations:

$$140 + 70*V = N$$

$$168 + 56*V = N,$$

Their solution is: N = 280 steps and V = 2 steps a second.

45. Three Actors

Three actors are getting ready for a performance. Two experienced make-up artists are working for them. Each actor should have a make-up and their hair should be brushed. Each actor's makeup takes 30 minutes, brushing takes only 10 minutes. How fast can these three actors get ready for coming on the stage?

Answer:

Getting ready will take 1 hour. For this hour the first make-up artist will have done faces for two actors (30 + 30 = 60 minutes), the other one will have done makeup for the third actor and will have brushed all three actors (10 + 30 + 10 + 10 = 60 minutes).

46. A King and a Minister

A king decided to unseat his minister without hurting his feelings. He invited the minister and suggested choosing one of the two pieces of paper, there was written "Stay" on one of them and "Go away" on the other one. The piece of paper pulled out by the minister would determine his fate. The minister figured out that it was written "Go away" on both pieces. Help the minister keep his seat!

Answer:

The minister can pull out a piece of paper and burn it without even looking at it. As far as it's written "Go away" on the other piece of paper, the king will have to admit that it was written "Stay" on the burnt piece of paper.

47. Six Glasses

There are six glasses in a row. The first three are full of water, the other three are empty. By moving only one glass you should arrange them so that empty and full glasses alternate.

Answer:

Pour the water from the second glass into the fifth glass.

48. Two Fathers and Two Sons

Two fathers and two sons ate 3 eggs for breakfast, each of them ate a whole egg. Could this happen?

Answer:

A grandfather, his son and grandson ate breakfast.

49. Two Wallets

There are two coins in two wallets. In one wallet there are twice as many coins as in the other one. Is this possible?

Answer:

It's possible. One wallet is inside the other.

50. Big Pots Season

When central heating and water heaters hadn't yet been invented, people usually heated water for taking a bath on kitchen stoves. Once a kitchen maid was heating water in a big pot on the stove to add it to the bath where there was already some amount of room-temperature water. Having noticed that, the butler told her, "Don't you understand that the longer you heat water on the stove, the colder the water in the bath is when you add heated water?" He was right. Why?

Answer:

The kitchen maid keeps boiling water on the stove, the water evaporates, and its volume decreases. The water in the bath still has room temperature. The more boiling water you add, the warmer the water in the bath is.